The
AVOCADO
Cookbook

The AVOCADO Cookbook

HENSLEY SPAIN

with illustrations by
JOANNA COLLARD

Wellington Lane Press Pty Ltd
Sydney   1977

Printed in Australia
by Southwood Press Pty Limited
80-92 Chapel Street, Marrickville, NSW
for Wellington Lane Press Pty Ltd
1 King George Street, McMahons Point, NSW 2060

National Library of Australia Cataloguing-in-Publication
data:

Spain, Hensley Reid, 1950-.
    The avocado cookbook.

    Index.
    ISBN 0 908022 01 8.

    1. Cookery (Avocado). I. Title.

641.6'4'653

Foreword

"And for you, sir?" asks the waiter, pencil poised.

"Avocado, please."

"How do you like it, sir? With vinaigrette or seafood?"

Waiters, and the chefs whose creations they bear to the board, seem never to have heard of Avocado Soufflé. Or Avocado Soup. Or Guacamole.

Nor to have considered that avocado served with freshly-squeezed orange juice, salt and ground pepper is perhaps preferable to avocado with vinegary dressing, the excessive acidity of which triumphantly obliterates the subtle, sensual, natural flavour of the fruit.

Hence the urgent need for a publication such as this.

A moratorium on Avocado Seafood and Avocado Vinaigrette, the Chocolate Mousse, Creme Caramel, Forbidden Apple and the dreaded Idaho Potato is clearly imminent. Pending which, alternative inspiration for at least the first two of these abominations can be found in the following pages.

To my good wishes to Hensley Spain for much success with this impressive collection of specialist recipes I add a fervent prayer that restauranteurs and cooks, both public and private, take it seriously enough to experiment with original new treatments of the admirable avocado, thereby affording the eating public a long anticipated and much needed relief from the two most favoured and most clichéed methods of preparation.

LEO SCHOFIELD

To Roger

Acknowledgements

I would like to thank the following people for their contributions to this book: Louise Ash, Hugh Beverley, the Collards, the Dettmanns, Lynsey Evans-Wardell, Anneliesje MacHunter, Raj Marwah, Shelley Moore, Susan Raehn, the Reids, the Spains, James Stevenson, Nick Truelove and Helen Zimmerman.

And I would especially like to thank Joanna Collard and Carol Dettmann — and Wellington Lane which was the physical link that allowed us to get and work together so well.

H.S.

Contents

Introduction

Avocados have two outstanding features:
• they are scrumptious;
• they are bursting with nutrients.

They are also, of course, expensive, only available for eight months of the year, and full of calories (or kilojoules for those readers who can cope with the metric system*). But these minor drawbacks fade when you realise how very many exciting ways there are to serve avocados, and how delicious the results can be.

So that you can discuss avocados authoritatively when your guests or family show interest as they enjoy one of your favourite recipes from this book, here is some background information on this most versatile, nutritious and delicious fruit.

Origins

The avocado is a member of the laurel family (Lauraceae), genus Persea; other members of the family are cinnamon, sassafras and camphor. It is native to tropical Central and South America. The Mexicans call the smooth yellowish-green pulp "butter growing on trees", and it is often used in their diet as it is in other countries of the region to which it is indigenous. In Guatemala, where the fruit is abundant during most of the year, it is one of the staple foods.

The English word avocado is derived from either the Spanish ahucato or aguacate, which in turn come from the Aztec ahuacatl. The avocado was first propagated by the Spanish in Jamaica after the Inquisition. Later, when the British occupied Jamaica, they were probably the first to associate the avocado with a pear, following the practice of early English colonists who ascribed characteristics of familiar fruits to previously unknown ones, such as custard apples or chinese gooseberries (now, in a further development, being marketed as kiwi fruit).

The fruit of the avocado tree varies in shape, size and colour. Avocados are usually pear-shaped, oval or ovoid. The colour of the skin varies from yellowish-green to dark green, maroon, reddish-brown and purplish-black. The skins can be thin and smooth or thick and pebbly. The fruit of some varieties is no larger than a good-sized olive, while others grow to more than 1.3 kg (three pounds).

Avocado trees are usually evergreen, though some varieties drop their leaves when the creamy blossoms appear.

---

* For those who can't cope yet, measurements in this book are given in cups, tablespoons, etc. Where the question cannot be begged, i.e. with weights and temperatures, both metric and imperial units are used.

Avocados in Australia

Fortunately, certain areas in Australia have a climate suited to the cultivation of avocados. Three main varieties are of commercial importance in Australia — the Fuerte, Shawill and Hass. The fruit of these self-pollinating varieties matures during different months, extending the availability of avocados from April to November.

Fuerte — Maturing in April, this hybrid of Mexican and Guatemalan origin is characterised by its distinctive soft, slightly pebbled green skin and elongated pear shape. The fruit is available until August. The flesh is smooth, with a high oil content and a rich flavour. The tree has low branches and a spreading growth.

Shawill — The Shawill variety crops more regularly than the Fuerte, which tends to be biennial, but not as heavily. The fruit generally matures from June to September. It is similar in colour and texture to the Fuerte, but tends to be more oval in shape. The trees are well shaped and can usually be recognised by their large, glossy leaves.

Hass — The latest of the three main varieties of avocado in Australia matures from August to November. Its thick, rough skin turns purplish-black when ripening. Trees of the Hass variety tend to grow upright, and the fruit is noted for its small seed.

Avocados do not ripen until they are harvested, and the fruit can be left on the tree for a while after it matures, so harvesting is not as critical as in many other fruit crops. But before you rush out to invest in an avocado plantation as an easy way to make your fortune, you should also be aware that the trees only bear after three or four years, and that they are very susceptible to Phytophtora cinnamoni, or root rot, which can cause extensive damage.

Nutritious as Well as Delicious

Next time you are feeling guilty about indulging in an avocado dish because of all the kilojoules/calories, you can console yourself by thinking of all the other important food elements it also contains. Half a large avocado — 100 g or 4 oz — has about 800 kj (190 calories) and 6 g of carbohydrate, but it also has 2 g of protein, 18 g of fat and 12 g of saturated fatty acid. Although the oil or fat content is about 20 per cent, it is unsaturated and in ideal proportions with saturated fats.

Avocados are low in starch (carbohydrate) and have almost no sugar. They are little gold mines of mineral deposits, however, with calcium, magnesium, potassium, sodium, phosphorus and iron. They also contain vitamins A, B_1, B_2, niacin, and vitamin C. And best of all, perhaps . . . they have no cholesterol.

Buying, Storing and Preparation

When you are buying avocados, look for the ones that are heavy, unbruised and are quite firm, or just beginning to soften. Avocados are ripe when gentle to moderate (for thicker skinned varieties) pressure applied to the skin results in a slight depression. (But please don't go around seeing how much pressure you can apply with a single thumb — you'll leave a legacy of bruised avocados for others.)

If avocados are purchased when they are hard, they will keep for weeks in the refrigerator and can be ripened at room temperature in a few days. To speed ripening, put them in a brown paper bag, or in a small drawer but remember that there is no way to make an avocado that is rock-hard in the morning ready for use that night, so some foresight is necessary. When fully ripe, the flesh of an avocado is soft, about the consistency of butter.

Use silver spoons or forks to scoop out or mash avocado flesh to prevent the discoloration and metallic taste that can occur from a chemical reaction with other metals.

Avocados should not be exposed to air for longer than necessary before serving as oxidation changes the taste and colour of the avocado — to prevent this, the avocado can be sprinkled with lemon or lime juice, or the stone can be left with the avocado until you are ready to serve it. Guacamole, for instance, can be made beforehand if the stone is buried in the mixture until you are ready to serve it.

Over-cooking can cause the avocado to become acid-tasting, and can also change the colour. Therefore in many of the soup recipes the avocado is added at the last moment — beware of trying to prepare the entire recipe in advance and reheating it before serving: many cooks have been astonished that the soup that tasted so terrific in the afternoon is such a bitter disaster when it is served at the dinner table.

You Don't Have to Eat Them

Finally, if you don't want to eat an avocado, you will find it can have other uses. It is excellent for the skin and hair, and makes an effective facial cleanser, moisturiser, and mask.

And you can grow a decorative house plant by suspending the base of an avocado stone (the round end nearest the stem) over water — or letting it stand in 2 – 3 cm (1 inch) of water — until it springs a root, and planting it in a good potting mixture.

The avocado is so versatile that it has no peer as a fruit. It can be enjoyed on its own or combined with a wide variety of foods to enhance the flavour and appearance of many dishes. I hope you will enjoy using this book as much as I have enjoyed writing it.

McMahons Point, Sydney   HENSLEY SPAIN

Starters

Canapés
Soups
Entrées

Canapés

- *Combine mashed avocado, shredded crab meat, finely chopped cucumber, and chopped shallots. Mix well. Spread on rounds of wholemeal toast.*

- *Combine diced avocados (sprinkled with lemon juice) and chopped artichoke hearts. Pour over french dressing and marinate for an hour. Serve on squares of wholemeal toast.*

- *Combine mashed avocado and cream cheese in a mixing bowl. Mix well. Spread on inside of celery stalks.*

Canapés

- Combine finely chopped school prawns, mashed avocado, lemon juice, and chopped chives. Mix well and spread on rounds of wholemeal toast.

- Combine 1 mashed avocado and 1 tablespoon mayonnaise. Mix well. Spread mixture on rounds of wholemeal toast. Top with crisp crumbed bacon.

- Combine mashed avocado, Worcestershire sauce, lemon juice, and onion salt. Mix well. Spread on rounds of wholemeal toast. Top with prawns, crab meat, chicken, cucumber, capsicum, etc.

Caviar Canapés

½ avocado (peeled, stoned and mashed)
 2 hard boiled eggs (sliced)
 2 small tomatoes (sliced)
 1 small onion (peeled and thinly sliced)
    black caviar
12 rounds of wholemeal toast

- Spread mashed avocado on toast rounds.
- Add layers of egg, tomato and onion on top of avocado.
- Top with caviar.

Fillet Canapé

12   thin slices of fillet (cooked and chilled)
12   rounds of wholemeal toast
      Avocado Spread (see below)
      caviar

- Cut fillet to fit toast rounds.
- Spread the toast with avocado spread, layer with fillet and top with caviar.

Avocado Spread

4   tablespoons mashed avocado
½   teaspoon Worcestershire sauce
1   teaspoon lemon juice
⅛   teaspoon garlic salt
½   teaspoon horseradish sauce

- Mix all ingredients well.

Hors D'oeuvres

- *Scoop out avocado balls and sprinkle with lemon juice. Place on toothpicks with cherry tomatoes.*

- *Scoop out avocado balls and sprinkle with lemon juice. Place on toothpicks with fried oysters.*

- *Dip avocado slices in French dressing. Roll slices of avocado in thin slices of ham.*

Avocado and Prosciutto

2   *medium avocados (peeled, stoned and cut into cubes)*
6   *paper-thin slices of prosciutto (cut into narrow strips)*
     juice of 1 lemon

- *Wrap the strips of prosciutto around the avocado cubes and secure with wooden toothpicks.*
- *Sprinkle with lemon juice.*

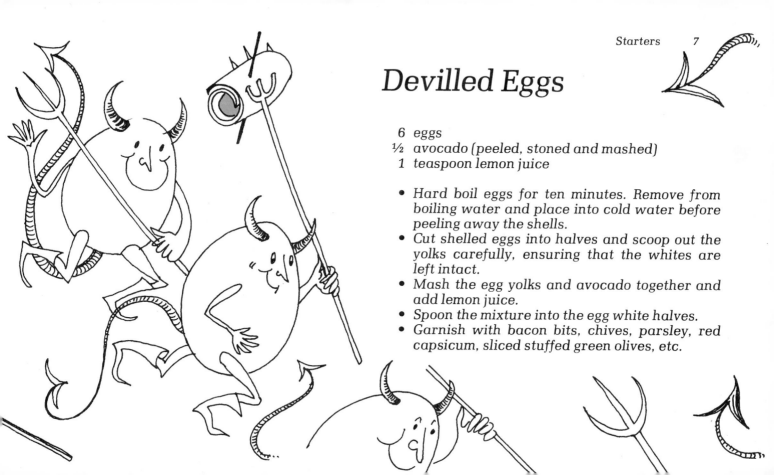

Devilled Eggs

6 eggs
½ avocado (peeled, stoned and mashed)
1 teaspoon lemon juice

- Hard boil eggs for ten minutes. Remove from boiling water and place into cold water before peeling away the shells.
- Cut shelled eggs into halves and scoop out the yolks carefully, ensuring that the whites are left intact.
- Mash the egg yolks and avocado together and add lemon juice.
- Spoon the mixture into the egg white halves.
- Garnish with bacon bits, chives, parsley, red capsicum, sliced stuffed green olives, etc.

Queensland Canapé

½ avocado (sliced)
12 rounds of wholemeal toast
 1 tablespoon mayonnaise
12 medium prawns (cooked and cleaned)
     pineapple pieces

- Spread toast rounds with mayonnaise.
- Put layers of prawn, pineapple and avocado slices on toast rounds. Put toothpicks through to hold canapés together.

Pacific Dip

1 large avocado (peeled, stoned and mashed)
½ cup sour cream
2 tablespoons shallots (finely chopped)
1 tablespoon chives (chopped)
¼ teaspoon cayenne pepper
2 tablespoons crab meat (cooked and shredded)
  paprika
  corn chips

- Mix together avocado, sour cream, shallots, chives, cayenne and crab meat.
- Put in serving bowl and sprinkle paprika over dip. Serve with corn chips or savoury biscuits.

Curry Crudité Dip

1   medium avocado (peeled, stoned and mashed)
2   tablespoons mayonnaise
½   teaspoon curry powder
1   tablespoon lemon juice
   carrot sticks
   celery sticks
   cauliflower pieces
   shallots

- Combine avocado, mayonnaise, curry powder and lemon juice. Mix well.
- Spoon avocado mixture into a serving dish and surround with carrots, celery, cauliflower and shallots.

Delta Dip

¾   cup crab meat (cooked and shredded)
1   tablespoon white wine
⅓   cup mayonnaise
½   avocado (puréed)
1   teaspoon French mustard
2   tablespoons parsley (chopped)
   sea salt and freshly ground black pepper to taste
   paprika

- Combine crab meat, white wine, mayonnaise, avocado purée, French mustard, parsley, sea salt and pepper. Mix well.
- Spoon into serving bowl and sprinkle paprika on top.
- Serve with savoury biscuits or corn chips.

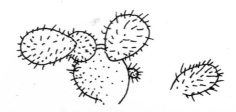

Guacamole

1 large avocado (peeled, stoned and mashed)
1 tomato (peeled and chopped)
1 tablespoon onion (finely chopped)
  a pinch of chili powder
¼ teaspoon dried coriander
¼ teaspoon garlic powder
  juice of ½ lemon
  vegetable salt to taste
  corn chips or savoury biscuits

- Combine all ingredients and mix well.
- Place the guacamole in a serving bowl.
- Serve with corn chips or savoury biscuits.
- Guacamole can also be served as a salad on a bed of lettuce.

Spinach and Avocado Soup

serves six

1 cup spinach (chopped and firmly packed)
1 avocado (peeled, stoned and chopped)
1 cup chicken broth
1 clove garlic (crushed)
2 tomatoes (peeled and chopped)
2 tablespoons lemon juice
  sea salt to taste
1 tablespoon chives (chopped)

- Combine spinach, avocado, chicken broth, garlic, tomatoes, lemon juice and sea salt in blender. Blend until smooth.
- Chill. Serve garnished with chives.

Avocado Vegetable Soup

serves four

1 small avocado (peeled, stoned and diced)
½ cup cucumber (diced)
2 tablespoons parsley
1 tomato (peeled and chopped)
½ cup celery (chopped)
2 tablespoons lemon juice
3 ice cubes
¼ cup shallots (chopped)

- Combine all ingredients but shallots in a blender and blend until smooth.
- Serve in individual soup bowls, garnished with chopped shallots.

Gazpacho

serves six

1   large tomato (finely chopped)
1   medium cucumber (peeled and finely chopped)
½   cup capsicum (finely chopped)
3   tablespoons onion (finely chopped)
1½   cups tomato juice
     juice of 1 lemon
2   tablespoons olive oil
1   clove garlic (crushed)
1   large avocado (peeled, stoned and diced)
     sea salt and freshly ground pepper to taste
     chopped parsley

- Combine tomato, cucumber, capsicum, onion, tomato juice, lemon juice, olive oil, and garlic in a bowl.
- Mix well and chill for two hours.
- Add avocado, cover, and chill for one hour more.
- Serve in individual bowls, garnished with parsley.

Iced Cucumber Soup

serves four

1   cup cucumber (peeled and chopped)
1   medium avocado (peeled, stoned and chopped)
1½   cups chicken stock
½   cup cream
2   tablespoons shallots (chopped)
2   tablespoons parsley (chopped)
1   tablespoon lemon juice
½   teaspoon sea salt
     paprika

- Combine cucumber, avocado, chicken stock, cream, shallots, parsley, lemon juice, and sea salt in a blender. Blend for 30 seconds.
- Chill for 1 hour.
- Serve in individual bowls. Sprinkle each with paprika.

Julep Soup

serves four

1 medium avocado (peeled, stoned and diced)
2 tins beef consommé
1 tablespoon lemon juice
2 tablespoons bourbon (or sherry)
1 dessertspoon mint (finely chopped)
   sea salt and freshly ground black pepper to taste

- Combine all ingredients and mix together until thoroughly blended.
- Chill for 3 to 4 hours, until soup is jellied.

Chilled Avocado Soup

serves four

1 large avocado
2 cups chicken stock
1 small onion (chopped)
1 tablespoon lemon juice
1 teaspoon sea salt
   freshly ground black pepper to taste
1 tablespoon tarragon (finely chopped)
1 tablespoon chives (chopped)
2 tablespoon parsley (finely chopped)

- Peel, stone and dice avocado.
- Combine diced avocado, chicken stock, chopped onion, lemon juice, sea salt and pepper. Place in a blender and blend until smooth.
- Add tarragon, chives and half the parsley and stir well. Cover and chill for one hour.
- Ladle into individual bowls and garnish with parsley.

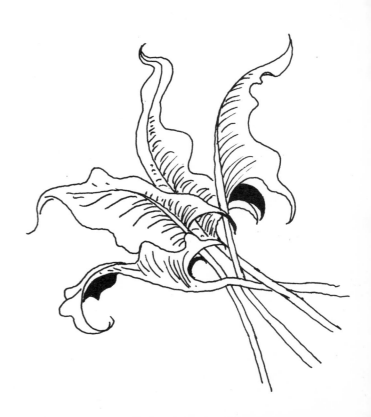

Fruit Soup

serves four to six

1   small avocado (peeled, stoned and diced)
½   cup banana (peeled and sliced)
½   cup pineapple (diced)
1   cup orange juice
4-6 orange slices

- Combine avocado, banana, pineapple and orange juice in a blender. Blend until smooth.
- Pour into individual soup bowls, and float orange slices on top.

Jellied Toheroa Soup

serves six

2 teaspoons gelatin
1 cup hot water
1 tin toheroa soup
   sea salt and freshly ground black pepper to
   taste
3 avocados
   juice of ½ lemon
4 teaspoons black caviar

- Dissolve gelatin in hot water, stirring continuously until dissolved.
- Combine gelatin, toheroa soup, sea salt and pepper. Mix and chill for three to four hours.
- Halve avocados, remove stones, and scoop out balls of avocado, being careful not to damage skins. Sprinkle avocado balls with lemon juice and put back into the avocado shells. Spoon jellied soup over balls.
- Top with caviar and serve.

Tomato and Avocado Soup

serves four

6 tomatoes (peeled and chopped)
1 cup milk
   juice of ½ lemon
2 tablespoons tomato paste
1 teaspoon honey
¾ teaspoon sea salt
⅛ teaspoon freshly ground black pepper
2 tablespoons parsley (finely chopped)
⅛ teaspoon garlic powder
1 medium avocado (peeled, stoned and diced)
4 teaspoons sour cream
   chopped chives

- Purée the tomatoes in a blender.
- In a bowl mix together the puréed tomatoes, milk, lemon juice and tomato paste.
- Stir in honey, sea salt, pepper, parsley and garlic powder.
- Refrigerate soup for a few hours.
- Shortly before serving add the diced avocado.
- Ladle soup into individual serving bowls and add a teaspoon of sour cream and a sprinkle of chives.

Seafood Bisque

serves six

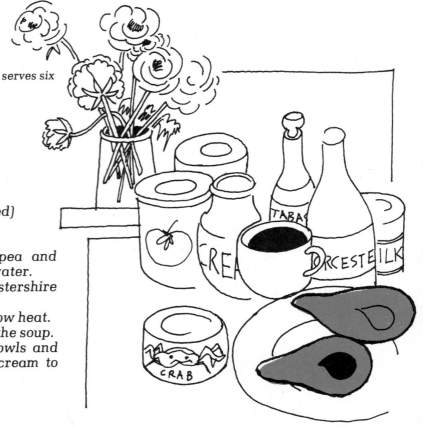

1 tin tomato soup
1 tin pea soup
4 cups water
1 small tin crab meat or lobster
   few drops Tabasco sauce
1 teaspoon Worcestershire sauce
1 small tin evaporated milk (chilled)
1 large avocado (peeled, stoned and diced)
   cream

- In a large saucepan combine the pea and tomato soups together with 4 cups of water.
- Add seafood, Tabasco and Worcestershire sauce.
- Simmer for at least 3 hours on a very low heat.
- Whip chilled evaporated milk. Add to the soup.
- Ladle soup into individual serving bowls and add diced avocado and 1 teaspoon cream to each bowl (do not stir in the cream).

Cream of Chicken Soup

serves six

1 tin mushroom soup
1 cup cooked chicken (diced)
1 cup chicken stock
1 cup milk
¼ teaspoon sea salt
1 medium avocado (peeled, stoned and cut into small cubes)
2 teaspoons lemon juice
  freshly ground black pepper
  chopped parsley

- Combine mushroom soup, chicken, chicken stock, milk, sea salt and black pepper in saucepan and simmer for ten minutes.
- Sprinkle cubes of avocado with lemon juice. Divide cubes equally and place in four soup bowls.
- Ladle soup into bowls.
- Garnish with parsley.

Ming Avocado

serves four

2   *small avocados (halved and stoned)*
½   *cup mandarin sections*
    Honey and Lemon Dressing (see below)

- *Fill avocado cavities with mandarin sections and serve with honey and lemon dressing*

Honey and Lemon Dressing

1   *tablespoon honey*
1   *tablespoon safflower oil*
    juice of ½ lemon
½   *teaspoon grated mandarin rind*

Avocados Rémoulade

serves six

3   *avocados (halved and stoned)*
2   *tablespoons lemon juice*
1½ *cups prawns (cooked and peeled)*
    Rémoulade Sauce

- *Sprinkle avocados with lemon juice.*
- *Cut prawns into bite-size pieces and spoon into avocado cavities.*
- *Spoon over Rémoulade Sauce.*

Rémoulade Sauce

½   *cup mayonnaise*
1   *tablespoon shallots (finely chopped)*
1   *tablespoon stuffed olives (chopped)*
1   *tablespoon parsley (chopped)*
1   *clove garlic (crushed)*
1   *teaspoon dry mustard*
1   *hard boiled egg (chopped)*

- *Combine all ingredients and chill.*

Crab Louis

serves six

Sauce Louis

3 medium avocados (halved and stoned)
½ lemon
¾ cup crab meat
1 hard boiled egg (chopped)
¼ cup celery (finely chopped)
lettuce
Sauce Louis (see below)

- Sprinkle stoned avocados with lemon juice.
- Combine cooked, shredded crab meat, egg and celery.
- Spoon crab meat mixture into avocado cavities.
- Spoon Sauce Louis over crab meat mixture.
- Serve on a bed of lettuce.

¼ cup mayonnaise
1 teaspoon chili sauce (more if desired)
2 teaspoons chives (chopped)
1 teaspoon lemon juice
4 tablespoons cream
1 stuffed olive (chopped)
½ teaspoon Worcestershire sauce
sea salt and freshly ground black pepper to taste

- Whip the cream and combine other ingredients in a separate bowl.
- Mix thoroughly and chill until ready to use.

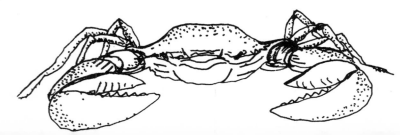

Avocado and Queensland Mudcrab

serves four

2 avocados (halved and stoned)
1 tablespoon lemon juice
¾ cup Queensland Mudcrab meat (cooked and shredded)
1 lemon

- Sprinkle the avocados with lemon juice.
- Fill the cavities with fresh crab ·meat.
- Garnish with lemon wedges.

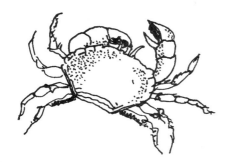

Chrissie's Oysters

serves four

24 oysters on the half-shell
 1 small avocado (mashed)
 2 tablespoons lime juice
 2 teaspoons onion (grated)
 1 tablespoon parsley (finely chopped)
    sea salt and freshly ground black pepper to
    taste

- Scrub and clean oyster shells.
- Combine mashed avocado, lime juice (or lemon juice if lime juice is not available), onion, parsley, sea salt and pepper. Mix well.
- Spoon avocado mixture onto oyster shells and place oysters on top.

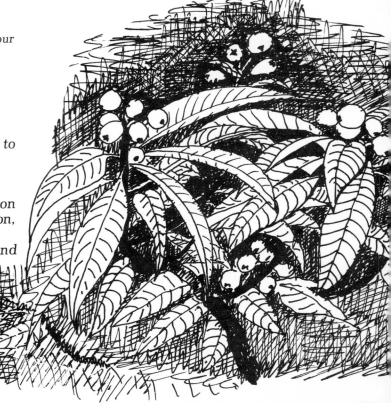

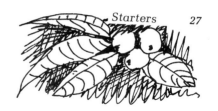

Camabiba Seafood Platter

serves four

12 mussels (washed, scraped and debearded)
¼ cup dry white wine
    lettuce leaves
1 medium avocado (peeled, stoned and sliced)
1 tablespoon lemon juice
8 shallot tops
2 medium tomatoes (cut into wedges)
8 oysters on the half-shell
8 king prawns (cooked and cleaned)
1 lemon (quartered)
    cocktail sauce

- Steam mussels open in white wine combined with ¼ cup water.
- Arrange lettuce leaves on four plates. Sprinkle avocado slices with lemon juice. Place avocado slices, shallot tops, and tomato wedges alternately on plates.
- Arrange mussels, oysters, and prawns on plates. Place cocktail sauce on lettuce leaf in the centre of the plate.
- Garnish with lemon wedges.

Mussels Jacqueline

serves four

24 fresh mussels
 3 rashers bacon
 1 bouquet garni
 1 tablespoon parsley (chopped)
½ cup white wine
 2 cloves garlic (crushed)
¼ cup shallots (very finely chopped)
 1 medium avocado (peeled, stoned and finely diced)
 2 tablespoons tomato sauce
½ cup breadcrumbs
    butter
    sea salt and freshly ground black pepper to taste

- Wash, scrape and debeard mussels.
- Grill bacon until crisp; place on brown paper or kitchen towelling to remove excess fat and then crumble into fine bits.
- Place mussels in a saucepan together with bouquet garni, chopped parsley and ½ cup white wine. Steam the mussels on a medium to hot flame until they open (about 8-10 minutes; discard any that do not open).
- Remove the mussels from their shells and put the shells aside for later use.
- In a separate pan, sauté shallots and crushed garlic in butter.
- Cut each of the mussels into about three pieces. Combine with the sautéed shallots and garlic and add avocado, tomato sauce and ¼ cup of the wine and parsley mixture in which the mussels cooked. Allow to simmer for 3 minutes.
- Spoon the mixture back into the mussel shells. Top with breadcrumbs, bacon bits and a nob of butter. Sprinkle with salt and pepper.
- Place under grill for 3 minutes and serve immediately.

Tomatoes Farci

serves four

4 medium tomatoes
4 tablespoons shallots (finely chopped)
1 small avocado (peeled, stoned and diced)
  sea salt and freshly ground black pepper to taste
  lettuce leaves
4 tablespoons mayonnaise
  prawns, crab meat or lobster (optional)

- Slice tops off tomatoes. Gently scoop out centres, being careful not to damage the skins.
- Combine tomato pulp, shallots, diced avocado, sea salt and pepper and seafood if desired. Mix well. Spoon mixture into tomato shells. Place tomatoes on beds of lettuce.
- Top with mayonnaise.

Prawn and Avocado Cocktail

serves four

2 medium avocados
1 cup fresh prawns (cooked and shelled)
4 tablespoons tomato sauce
1 tablespoon mayonnaise
1 teaspoon horseradish sauce
1 teaspoon Worcestershire sauce
2 drops Tabasco sauce
   juice of 1 lemon
½ teaspoon vegetable salt
   freshly ground black pepper
   lettuce

- Combine tomato sauce, mayonnaise, horseradish, Worcestershire sauce, lemon juice, Tabasco, salt and pepper.
- Peel, stone and scoop out balls of avocado (or cut the avocado flesh into cubes).
- Combine avocado balls with bite-size chunks of prawn.
- Place the prawn and avocado mixture on a bed of lettuce in individual serving bowls, then spoon some sauce on each serving.
- Garnish with lemon wedges.

Lunches

Salads
Egg Dishes
Sandwiches

Neptune Salad

serves three to four

1 large avocado (peeled, stoned and sliced)
2 tomatoes (cut into wedges)
1 cup school prawns (cooked and cleaned)
8 stuffed olives (halved)
1 small head of lettuce
1 tablespoon chives (chopped)
6 anchovy fillets
1 hard boiled egg (sliced)
  Tarragon Dressing (see below)

- Tear lettuce into bite-size pieces.
- Combine lettuce with sliced avocado, tomatoes, prawns, olives and chopped chives in a salad bowl. Pour dressing over and toss.
- Arrange anchovies and egg slices alternately on top of salad.

Tarragon Dressing

4 tablespoons olive oil
2 tablespoons tarragon vinegar
¼ teaspoon paprika
  sea salt and freshly ground black pepper to taste

- Combine ingredients in a jar and shake well.

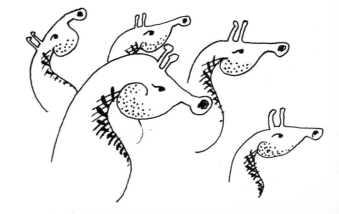

Cornucopia

serves six

1½ cups prawns
1 small tin tiny corn
6 artichoke hearts (chopped)
1 tomato (cut into wedges)
½ cucumber (peeled and diced)
1 small head of lettuce
1 avocado (peeled, stoned and diced)
   Dressing (see below)

- Clean prawns and cut into bite-size pieces.
- Combine prawn pieces with drained corn, artichoke hearts, tomato wedges, diced cucumber and avocados.
- Tear lettuce into small pieces and toss with other ingredients and dressing in a salad bowl.

Dressing

4 tablespoons olive oil
2 tablespoons white vinegar
2 teaspoons honey
1 clove garlic (crushed)
   sea salt and freshly ground black pepper to taste

- Combine all ingredients in a jar and shake well.

Prawn Salad

serves four

1 cup prawns (cooked)
1 large avocado (peeled, stoned and diced)
1 cup celery (chopped)
¼ cup onion (finely chopped)
1 cup cucumber (peeled and chopped)
½ cup capsicum (finely chopped)
6 tablespoons mayonnaise
½ teaspoon sea salt
1 head lettuce
4 tomatoes (quartered)
4 lemon wedges

- Peel prawns and cut into bite-size pieces.
- Combine prawns with diced avocado and chopped celery, onion, cucumber and capsicum. Mix well.
- Stir in mayonnaise and sea salt.
- Serve on a bed of lettuce with quartered tomatoes.
- Garnish with lemon wedges.

Lobster Capers

serves six

1½ cups lobster (cooked and diced)
 ½ cup celery
  6 tablespoons mayonnaise
  3 avocados (peeled, stoned and halved)
     juice of ½ lemon
  1 head lettuce
  2 tablespoons capers (chopped)

- Combine lobster, celery and mayonnaise in a mixing bowl. Mix well.
- Place halved avocados onto beds of lettuce on individual luncheon plates.
- Spoon lobster salad over avocados.
- Garnish with capers.

Uncle Joe's Salad

serves four

1 cup cold cooked roast beef
1 large avocado (peeled, stoned and sliced)
1 cucumber (peeled and diced)
2 tablespoons shallots (chopped)
  lettuce
  Horseradish Dressing (see below)

- Cut beef into bite-size pieces.
- Combine roast beef with sliced avocado, diced cucumber and chopped shallots.
- Add Horseradish Dressing and mix well.
- Spoon salad onto bed of lettuce.

Horseradish Dressing

6 tablespoons mayonnaise
1 teaspoon horseradish (grated)
  pinch of paprika

- Combine ingredients and mix thoroughly.

Avocado Chicken Salad

serves four

1 avocado (peeled, stoned and sliced)
1 cup chicken (cooked and diced)
1 cup apple (peeled, cored and diced)
½ cup celery (finely chopped)
¼ cup onion (finely chopped)
2 tablespoons almonds (slivered)
4 tomatoes
4 tablespoons mayonnaise
 celery salt to taste
 lettuce
 parsley

- *Combine diced chicken and apple with chopped celery and onion and slivered almonds in a mixing bowl. Mix well.*
- *Add mayonnaise and mix thoroughly. Sprinkle with celery salt.*
- *Cut the centres out of the tomatoes with a sharp knife and almost quarter the tomatoes.*
- *Place tomatoes on a bed of lettuce on individual plates.*
- *Spoon chicken salad over tomatoes.*
- *Place avocado slices around each tomato.*
- *Garnish with parsley.*

Avocado, Turkey and Caviar

serves six

1 cup turkey (cooked and diced)
⅓ cup celery (chopped)
1 tablespoon onion (grated)
3 avocados (halved and stoned)
  juice of ½ lemon
  lettuce
  Thousand Island Dressing (see below)
6 teaspoons caviar

- Sprinkle avocados with lemon juice.
- Combine diced turkey, chopped celery and grated onion.
- Place avocado halves on beds of lettuce on individual luncheon plates.
- Spoon turkey mixture into avocado cavities.
- Pour over Thousand Island Dressing.
- Top each serving with a teaspoonful of caviar.

Thousand Island Dressing

4 tablespoons mayonnaise
1 teaspoon chili sauce
3 tablespoons tomato sauce
2 teaspoons celery (finely chopped)
1 teaspoon green olives (finely chopped)
1 teaspoon dill pickle (finely chopped)

- Mix ingredients and chill.

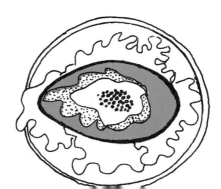

Duck and Cashew Salad

serves six

1½   cups duck (cooked and diced)
⅓   cup pineapple (finely chopped)
¼   cup celery (chopped)
¼   cup apple (cored and chopped)
½   cup unsalted roasted cashews (chopped)
2   tablespoons shallots (finely chopped)
1   tablespoon sherry
4   tablespoons mayonnaise
3   avocados (halved and stoned)
6   sprigs parsley
    lettuce

- Combine duck with chopped pineapple, celery, apple, cashews, shallots and dry sherry in a mixing bowl. Mix well.
- Add mayonnaise and stir thoroughly.
- Place avocado halves on beds of lettuce on individual luncheon plates.
- Spoon duck salad over avocados and garnish with parsley.

Avocado Waldorf

serves four

1 medium avocado (peeled, stoned and diced)
2 teaspoons lemon juice
1 cup apple (cored and diced)
½ cup celery (chopped)
1 cup lettuce (torn into bite-size pieces)
6 tablespoons mayonnaise
½ cup walnuts (chopped)

- Sprinkle diced avocado with lemon juice and combine with diced apple and chopped celery in a mixing bowl.
- Add mayonnaise and mix well.
- Add walnuts and mix thoroughly.
- Serve on bed of lettuce.

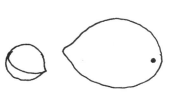

Thanksgiving Salad

serves four

8 slices cooked turkey
4 tablespoons whole berry cranberry sauce
1 avocado (peeled, stoned and sliced)
   lettuce

- *Place beds of lettuce on four salad plates.*
- *Put slices of turkey and avocado on top of lettuce.*
- *Spoon over cranberry sauce.*

Cobb Salad

serves four

Russian Dressing

4 bacon rashers
1 medium head lettuce (torn into bite-size pieces)
1 cup watercress
½ cup capsicum (cut in strips)
3 medium tomatoes (cut in wedges)
1 small cucumber (peeled and sliced)
2 medium avocados (peeled, stoned and sliced)
1½ cups chicken (cooked and diced)
1 tablespoon shallots (finely chopped)
Russian Dressing (see below)

- Grill bacon until crisp. Drain on brown paper or kitchen towelling and crumble into bits.
- Combine lettuce, watercress, capsicum, tomatoes, cucumber, avocados, chicken and shallots.
- Toss and serve in four large salad bowls. Top with Russian Dressing and sprinkle with bacon.

6 tablespoons mayonnaise
2 tablespoons tomato sauce
2 teaspoons chili sauce
2 tablespoons lemon juice
2 tablespoons capsicum (finely chopped)
2 tablespoons chives (chopped)
2 teaspoons pimento (chopped)

- Combine all ingredients and mix well.

Bilpin Salad

serves six

1½ cups pork (cooked and cubed)
3   avocados (halved and stoned)
Apple Sauce (see below)

- Spoon chilled pork over avocado.
- Top with apple sauce.

Apple Sauce

3 Granny Smith apples
2 tablespoons raw sugar
2 tablespoons water

- Peel, core and dice apples. Put in saucepan with sugar and water.
- Cook over low heat until apples are broken up. Cool.

Chef Salad

serves four

1 small head of lettuce
½ cup celery (chopped)
½ cup carrots (grated)
1 cucumber (peeled and sliced)
2 tomatoes (cut into wedges)
2 tablespoons shallots (chopped)
¼ cup capsicum (cut in strips)
1 small avocado (peeled, stoned and sliced)
   strips of cooked ham or turkey
1 hard boiled egg (chilled)
   Chef Dressing (see below)

- Tear lettuce into bite-size pieces and combine in a salad bowl with chopped celery, grated carrots, sliced cucumber, tomato wedges, chopped shallots and capsicum strips. Mix well.
- Decorate the top with slices of avocado, strips of meat, and slices of hard boiled egg.
- Pour over dressing.

Dressing

4 tablespoons olive oil
2 tablespoons vinegar
2 teaspoons honey
2 teaspoons lemon juice
½ teaspoon paprika
½ teaspoon sea salt

- Combine all ingredients and stir with spoon until honey is well blended.

Tomato Aspic

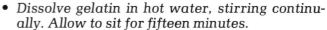

serves four

3   teaspoons gelatin
½   cup hot water
1½ cups tomato juice
½   teaspoon onion salt
    freshly ground black pepper to taste
1   small avocado (peeled, stoned and sliced and
    sprinkled with lemon juice)
½   cup celery (finely chopped)
2   tablespoons stuffed olives (sliced)
    lettuce leaves
    mayonnaise

- Dissolve gelatin in hot water, stirring continually. Allow to sit for fifteen minutes.
- Combine tomato juice, onion salt, pepper and gelatin. Mix well.
- Pour half the tomato mixture into oiled mould. Place in refrigerator. When it begins to set add half the avocados, celery and olives. Pour over the remaining tomato juice mixture and return to refrigerator.
- Add remaining ingredients when it begins to set and chill until firmly set.
- Turn mould onto lettuce leaves and top with mayonnaise.

Avocado Aspic

serves four

1 package lemon flavoured jelly crystals
2 cups hot water
1 small avocado (peeled, stoned, and sliced)
1 tablespoon lemon juice

- Pour jelly crystals into bowl.
- Add hot water (not boiling) and stir until dissolved.
- Put half the jelly into a medium size mould and chill until set.
- Place avocado slices on top of set jelly and pour over the remaining cooled jelly. Chill until set and serve.

Fillings for Avocados

Potato Filling

serves four

¼ cup lettuce (shredded)
½ cup potatoes (cooked, diced and chilled)
1 rasher of bacon (grilled crisp and crumbled)
1 teaspoon mint (finely chopped)
1 tablespoon shallots (finely chopped)
2 tablespoons mayonnaise
2 avocados (halved and stoned)

• Combine lettuce, potatoes, bacon, mint, shallots and mayonnaise. Mix well. Spoon into avocado halves.

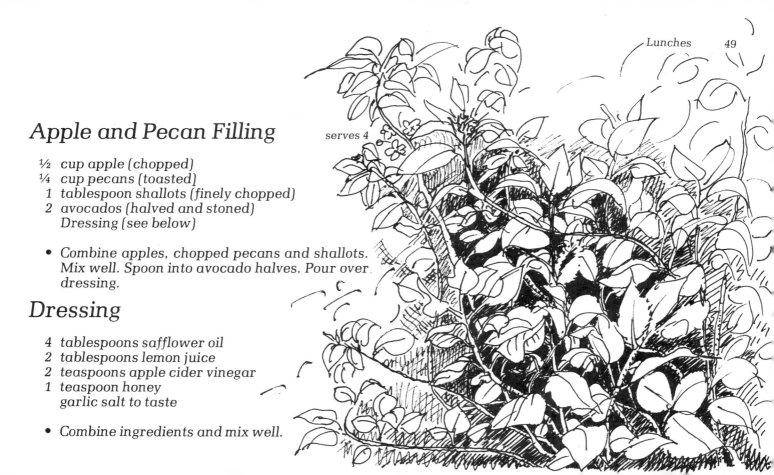

Apple and Pecan Filling

serves 4

½ cup apple (chopped)
¼ cup pecans (toasted)
1 tablespoon shallots (finely chopped)
2 avocados (halved and stoned)
Dressing (see below)

- *Combine apples, chopped pecans and shallots. Mix well. Spoon into avocado halves. Pour over dressing.*

Dressing

4 tablespoons safflower oil
2 tablespoons lemon juice
2 teaspoons apple cider vinegar
1 teaspoon honey
garlic salt to taste

- *Combine ingredients and mix well.*

Marinated Beef Salad

serves four

1 large avocado (peeled, stoned and sliced)
1 tablespoon lemon juice
1½ cups fillet steak (cooked and cut in bite-size pieces)
1 medium onion (thinly sliced)
2 tomatoes (sliced)
2 tablespoons parsley (chopped)
Dressing (see below)

- Sprinkle avocado slices with lemon juice.
- In a casserole, stack layers of beef, onion, tomatoes, avocado and parsley.
- Pour over dressing, cover and marinate for at least one hour before serving.

Dressing

½ cup safflower oil
juice of 1 lemon
1 tablespoon apple cider vinegar
1 teaspoon dry mustard
1 teaspoon sea salt
freshly ground black pepper to taste
½ teaspoon oregano
1 garlic clove (crushed)

- Combine ingredients and mix well.

Avocado Quiche

serves four to six

1   unbaked pastry shell
3   eggs
½   cup cream
½   cup milk
½   teaspoon nutmeg
1   medium avocado (mashed)
2   teaspoons lemon juice
1   teaspoon French mustard
¼   teaspoon sea salt
⅛   teaspoon freshly ground black pepper
3   tablespoons onion (finely chopped)
3   rashers bacon (diced)
¾   cup Swiss cheese (grated)

- Preheat oven to 175°C (350°F).
- Combine eggs, cream, milk, nutmeg, mashed avocado sprinkled with lemon juice, mustard, sea salt and pepper. Beat until smooth.
- Fry onion and bacon lightly in frying pan. Remove from pan and set aside.
- Sprinkle bottom of pastry shell with half the onion and bacon mixture and half the cheese.
- Pour in egg and avocado mixture. Sprinkle remainder of onion and bacon and cheese on top.
- Bake for 25-30 minutes.

Avocado Omelet

serves four

6   eggs
⅔   cup milk
    sea salt and freshly ground black pepper
2   tablespoons cheddar cheese (grated)
1   small onion (chopped)
1   tablespoon butter
1   medium tomato (peeled and chopped)
1   small avocado (peeled, stoned and sliced)

- *Separate 3 eggs. Beat the whites until light and fluffy. Mix in the other 3 yolks and 3 eggs with a whisk.*
- *Add milk, sea salt, pepper and grated cheese.*
- *Put butter in frying pan on medium heat, and when pan is hot pour in half the mixture. Cook one side, then turn and cook on the other side. Repeat the process with the remaining mixture.*
- *Slice each omelet in half and place on individual plates. Top with onion, tomato and slices of avocado.*

Avocado Soufflé

serves four

1   tablespoon butter
1   tablespoon wholemeal flour
½   cup milk
¼   cup cheddar cheese (grated)
     sea salt and freshly ground black pepper to
     taste
2   eggs (separated)
½   cup avocado purée

- Preheat oven to 175°C (350°F).
- Melt butter in saucepan and blend in flour. Cook over low heat, stirring constantly, for 2 to 3 minutes.
- Add milk, cheese, salt and pepper, and continue stirring until sauce has thickened.
- Allow to cool slightly and add beaten egg yolks.
- Stir in avocado purée and set aside.
- Beat egg whites in a mixing bowl until stiff but not dry.
- Gently fold egg whites into avocado mixture.
- Pour into a well-greased baking dish and bake for 35 minutes.
- Serve immediately.

South of the Border

serves four

8 taco shells
1 cup chili con carne (page 101)
1 cup shredded lettuce
¾ cup cheddar cheese (grated)
   guacamole (page 11)

- Spoon chili con carne into taco shell. Top with shredded lettuce, cheddar cheese and guacamole.

Huevos Rancheros

serves four

4   tortillas
¾   cup onions (chopped)
¼   cup capsicum (chopped)
½   cup eggplant (peeled and chopped) (optional)
3   tablespoons butter
1   cup tomatoes (peeled and chopped)
2   teaspoons chili sauce
2   tablespoons tomato sauce
    sea salt and freshly ground black pepper to taste
4   eggs
½   cup milk
1   medium avocado (peeled, stoned and sliced)

- Fry tortillas.
- Cook onions, capsicum and eggplant, if desired, in 2 tablespoons butter until onions are transparent. Add tomatoes, chili sauce, tomato sauce, sea salt and pepper. Cook gently for 15-20 minutes or until sauce thickens.
- Combine eggs and milk in a mixing bowl and beat thoroughly.
- Add sea salt and pepper to taste.
- Melt butter in a frying pan, add egg mixture and cook over low to medium heat, stirring continuously until done.
- Spoon sauce over tortillas. Place scrambled eggs on top of sauce on each tortilla.
- Garnish with avocado slices and serve while eggs are hot.

Avocado Scramble

serves four

2 bacon rashers
4 eggs (beaten)
½ cup milk
  sea salt and freshly ground black pepper to taste
1 small avocado (peeled, stoned, diced)
2 teaspoons butter
4 pieces wholemeal toast

- Grill bacon until crisp, drain and crumble.
- Combine eggs and milk in a mixing bowl and beat thoroughly.
- Add sea salt and pepper to taste.
- Melt butter in a frying pan, add egg mixture and cook over a low to medium heat, stirring continuously until done.
- Add diced avocado and serve on toast, topped with crumbled bacon.

Earl's Sandwich

serves four

4 slices roast beef
   mayonnaise
¼ cucumber (thinly sliced)
1 small onion (thinly sliced)
1 medium avocado (peeled, stoned and sliced)
4 wholemeal buns (halved)

- Spread mayonnaise on halved wholemeal buns.
- Add roast beef, cucumber, onion and avocado.

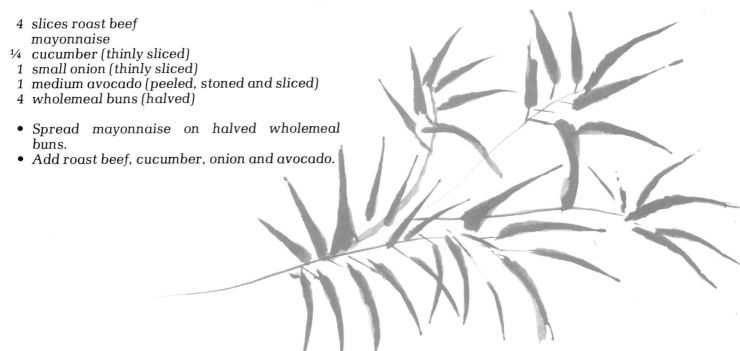

Avocado and Cream Cheese Sandwich

serves four

1   small avocado (mashed)
6   tablespoons cream cheese
1   tablespoon lemon juice
4   stuffed olives (chopped)
1   tablespoon parsley (chopped)
½   cucumber (peeled and sliced)
8   slices of wholemeal bread

- Toast bread.
- Combine mashed avocado, cream cheese, lemon juice, olives and parsley. Mix well.
- Spread onto wholemeal toast. Arrange cucumber slices on top.
- Cut sandwiches into quarters.

The Crispy Goodness Sandwich

serves four

2 tablespoons sultanas
1 tablespoon shallots (finely chopped)
2 tablespoons mayonnaise
1 tablespoon celery (finely chopped)
1 medium avocado (peeled, stoned and sliced)
½ cup bean sprouts
8 slices of wholemeal bread

- Combine sultanas, shallots, mayonnaise, and celery. Mix well.
- Spread on four slices of bread.
- Top with avocado slices and bean sprouts.

Beef Relish Sandwich

serves four

4   slices of roast beef
4   tablespoons corn relish
   lettuce leaves
1   small avocado (peeled, stoned and sliced)
2   tablespoons butter
   sea salt to taste
8   slices of rye bread

- Spread butter on four slices of rye bread.
- Layer lettuce leaves, slices of roast beef, and slices of avocado on rye bread. Top with corn relish. Season to taste with sea salt.

Monday Sandwich

serves four

2 tablespoons butter
4 slices cooked lamb
2 tablespoons fruit chutney
   lettuce leaves
1 medium avocado (peeled, stoned and sliced)
8 slices wholemeal bread

- Spread butter on four slices of bread.
- Layer lettuce leaves, lamb, fruit chutney and avocado slices on bread.

Bilpin Sandwich

serves four

 8 slices of wholemeal bread
 2 tablespoons butter
    lettuce leaves
 4 slices cooked pork
 1 small avocado (peeled, stoned and sliced)
½ cup apple (grated or finely chopped)

- Toast bread.
- Spread four slices of toast with butter.
- Layer lettuce leaves, slices of pork, apple and avocado slices on toast.

Tuesday Sandwich

serves four

4 slices cooked lamb
   mint jelly
1 small avocado (mashed)
   garlic salt to taste
   lettuce leaves
8 slices of wholemeal bread

- Toast bread.
- Spread mashed avocado on four slices of toasted bread. Sprinkle with garlic salt.
- Layer lettuce leaves and slices of lamb on toast. Top with mint jelly.

Neopolitan Sandwich

serves four

2 tablespoons safflower oil
2 tablespoons butter
1 medium onion (peeled and chopped)
1 clove garlic (crushed)
2 cups topside mince
¼ cup dry white wine
½ cup tomato paste
2 beef stock cubes
½ cup water
¼ cup capsicum (chopped)
¼ cup celery (chopped)
½ teaspoon oregano
   bay leaf
1 teaspoon raw sugar
   sea salt and freshly ground black pepper to taste
2 medium avocados (peeled, stoned and sliced)
4 pieces of wholemeal bread (toasted)

- Heat oil and butter in frying pan. Brown onion, garlic and minced meat.
- Add white wine, tomato paste, beef stock cubes dissolved in hot water, capsicum, celery, oregano, bay leaf, sugar, sea salt and pepper. Allow to simmer for 1 hour.
- Arrange sliced avocados on toasted bread. Spoon over meat sauce and serve immediately.

Natasha's Prawn Sandwich

serves four

2 bacon rashers
2 cups school prawns (cooked and cleaned)
1 large avocado (peeled, stoned and sliced)
   lettuce leaves
   Russian Dressing (see below)
4 lemon wedges
4 slices of pumpernickel bread

- Grill bacon until crisp and drain on brown paper or kitchen towelling.
- Place slices of pumpernickel on individual plates. Put lettuce leaves on each piece of bread.
- Arrange avocado slices on lettuce.
- Spoon on prawns. Pour over Russian Dressing and top with crumbled bacon.
- Garnish with lemon wedges.

Russian Dressing

¼ cup tomato sauce
¼ cup mayonnaise
2 tablespoons celery (finely chopped)
1 tablespoon chives (chopped)
1 tablespoon caviar (optional)

- Combine ingredients and mix well.

Gobbley Sandwich

serves four

4   bacon rashers
    mayonnaise
    lettuce leaves
4   slices cooked turkey
1   large avocado (peeled, stoned and sliced)
8   slices of wholemeal bread

- Grill four rashers of bacon until crisp. Place on brown paper or kitchen towelling to drain.
- Toast bread.
- Spread mayonnaise on four slices of toasted bread.
- Put on layers of lettuce leaves, turkey, avocado and bacon.

Mr McGregor's Sandwich

serves four

4   slices cooked chicken
    lettuce leaves
¼   cup carrot (grated)
    mayonnaise
1   small onion (thinly sliced)
1   small avocado (peeled, stoned and sliced)
8   slices of wholemeal bread

- Toast bread.
- Spread mayonnaise on four slices of toast.
- Put layers of lettuce leaves, chicken, avocado and onion on toast. Top with grated carrot.

Atlantean Sandwich

serves four

 4 slices cooked turkey
 1 tomato (sliced)
    lettuce leaves
 1 medium avocado (peeled, stoned and sliced)
    mayonnaise
12 slices of wholemeal bread

- Toast bread.
- Spread each slice of toast with mayonnaise.
- Place lettuce leaves and chicken slices on four pieces of toast. Top with toast and then add tomato slices and avocado slices.
- Complete each sandwich with third slice of toast, quarter sandwiches and keep together with toothpicks.

The B.L.T. Avocado

serves four

4   bacon rashers
1   medium avocado (mashed)
1   large tomato (sliced)
    lettuce leaves
8   slices wholemeal bread (toasted)

- Grill four rashers of bacon until crisp. Place on brown paper or kitchen towelling to drain.
- Toast bread, then spread 4 slices with mashed avocado.
- Add layers of lettuce leaves, bacon and tomato.

Carolina Sandwich

serves four

½ cup crab meat
2 tablespoons mayonnaise
1 tablespoon shallots (finely chopped)
3 tablespoons cucumber (chopped)
1 small avocado (mashed)
   lettuce leaves
8 slices wholemeal bread

- Toast bread.
- Combine mayonnaise, shallots, cucumber, and mashed avocado. Mix well.
- Spread onto four slices of toasted bread.
- Layer lettuce leaves on toast. Spoon crab meat onto lettuce leaves.

Sunset Sandwich

serves four

8 slices wholemeal bread
2 tablespoons mayonnaise
½ cup red salmon
2 hard boiled eggs (sliced)
1 small avocado (peeled, stoned and sliced)
   lettuce leaves

- Toast bread.
- Spread mayonnaise onto four slices of toast.
- Layer toast with lettuce leaves, salmon and egg slices and top with avocado slices.

Steak Sandwich

serves six

6 thin steaks
6 wholemeal buns
3 tablespoons butter
1 cup shredded lettuce
3 tablespoons chili sauce (page 101)
¾ cup cheddar cheese (grated)
1 medium avocado (mashed)

- *Grill steaks.*
- *Spread butter on halved wholemeal buns and brown under griller.*
- *Spread mashed avocado on bottom halves of four buns. Cover with lettuce and put steaks on buns, add chili sauce and sprinkle with cheddar cheese.*

A Longueville Lunch

4   slices ham (cooked)
1   medium avocado (mashed)
4   slices pineapple
½   cup coleslaw
8   slices wholemeal bread

- *Toast bread.*
- *Spread mashed avocado onto four pieces of toast.*
- *Add layers of ham and pineapple. Top with coleslaw.*

Cosmopolitan Sandwich

serves four

8   slices cooked chicken
    mayonnaise
1   medium tomato (sliced)
4   thin slices onion
4   tablespoons bean sprouts
1   tablespoon parsley (chopped)
1   medium avocado (peeled, stoned and sliced)
8   slices wholemeal bread

- Toast bread.
- Spread four slices of wholemeal toast with mayonnaise.
- Layer chicken, tomato, onion, bean sprouts, parsley, and avocado on top.

Spreads for Sandwiches

1   small avocado (mashed)
½   clove garlic (crushed)
1   teaspoon lemon juice
1   tablespoon shallots (finely chopped)
1   tablespoon parsley (finely chopped)
    pinch of chili powder
    sea salt to taste

• Combine all ingredients and mix well.

1   small avocado (mashed)
¼   cup cheddar cheese (grated)
1   tablespoon parsley (finely chopped)
1   tablespoon sour cream
1   teaspoon Worcestershire sauce
1   tablespoon chives (chopped)
1   teaspoon lemon juice

• Combine all ingredients and mix well.

More Sandwich Suggestions

- sliced avocado, sea salt, pepper and lemon juice on wholemeal bread
- ham, avocado slices and french mustard
- chicken slices, toasted almonds, avocado slices, lettuce and mayonnaise
- roast beef, avocado slices and prepared horseradish sauce
- mashed avocado, cucumber slices and watercress
- roast beef, coleslaw and avocado slices
- hamburger, onion slices and mashed avocado
- cucumber slices, capsicum strips, avocado slices, mayonnaise and chopped walnuts
- mashed avocados and baked beans
- mashed avocados and mashed bananas

Main Courses

Louise's Fillet of Beef with Avocado Sauce

serves six

1.5 kg (3½ lb) fillet of beef
   4 garlic cloves (sliced)
   3 tablespoons oil
      Avocado Sauce (see below)

- Preheat oven to 190°C (375°F).
- Fry sliced garlic cloves in oil until light golden.
- Place fillet of beef in baking pan. Pour over half the oil and garlic. Roast for 30 to 35 minutes, basting with remaining oil and garlic occasionally.
- Slice and serve with avocado sauce.

Avocado Sauce

1 large avocado
2 tablespoons cream
   sea salt and freshly ground black pepper
   pinch of nutmeg
1 tablespoon olive oil
1 teaspoon lemon juice

- Peel, stone and mash avocado. Add cream, nutmeg, olive oil and lemon juice. Mix well.
- Season to taste with sea salt and pepper.

Avocado Schnitzel

serves six

2 cups veal steak (thin slices, cut in finger-length strips)
½ cup wholemeal flour
2 eggs (beaten)
½ cup breadcrumbs
   sea salt and freshly ground black pepper to taste
2 tablespoons butter
2 tablespoons oil
2 medium avocados (peeled, stoned and sliced)
1 lemon
6 sprigs of parsley

- Season veal steak with sea salt and pepper. Dip veal in flour, then egg mixture, and then breadcrumbs.
- Sauté veal in melted butter and oil until crisp.
- Place avocado slices on individual plates and top with veal steak. Sprinkle lemon juice and garnish with parsley.

Leg of Lamb with Minted Avocado Sauce

serves six

2 kg (4½ lb) leg of lamb
3 tablespoons wholemeal flour
2 garlic cloves
4 tablespoons bacon fat
   Minted Avocado Sauce (see below)

- Preheat oven to 190°C (375°F).
- Sprinkle the wholemeal flour in a baking dish.
- Cut each garlic clove into four slivers and insert in lamb.
- Place lamb in baking dish and baste with bacon fat.
- Bake for 1¾ hours. Serve with minted avocado sauce.

Minted Avocado Sauce

1 large avocado (peeled, stoned and mashed)
   juice of ½ lemon
1 tablespoon mint (very finely chopped)
1 clove of garlic (crushed)
   sea salt to taste

- Combine ingredients and mix well.

Karabella Chicken

serves six

1　large chicken cut into six pieces
½　teaspoon paprika
　　sea salt and freshly ground black pepper to taste
6　tablespoons butter
2　tablespoons safflower oil
1　cup pineapple (chopped into bite-size pieces)
1　medium avocado (peeled, stoned and sliced)
3　rashers bacon (grilled crisp and crumbled)

- Preheat oven to 190°C (375°F).
- Place each piece of chicken on a square of aluminium foil. Sprinkle with paprika, salt and pepper. Add a dab of butter.
- Wrap in foil and cook in oven for 1 hour.
- Shortly before serving heat oil in a frying pan. Add pineapple pieces and cook gently for five minutes.
- Unwrap chicken, place on individual plates and spoon over pineapple pieces. Top with avocado slices and garnish with crumbled bacon. Serve immediately.

Avocado and Chicken with Almonds

serves six

6 chicken breasts
3 tablespoons wholemeal flour
½ teaspoon paprika
2 tablespoons oil
2 onions (finely chopped)
1 clove garlic (crushed)
2 medium tomatoes (peeled and chopped)
1 cup dry white wine
½ cup mushrooms (sliced)
   sea salt and freshly ground black pepper to taste
¼ cup slivered almonds
2 tablespoons butter
1 large avocado (peeled, stoned and sliced)
1 tablespoon lemon juice

- Preheat oven to 175°C (350°F).
- Dip chicken pieces in flour mixed with paprika. In a large frying pan brown the chicken pieces in oil. Remove chicken pieces from frying pan.
- Add the onions and garlic to frying pan and cook until onions are transparent.
- Add tomatoes, white wine, mushrooms, sea salt and pepper. Simmer for five minutes.
- Place chicken pieces in a casserole. Pour over tomato/mushroom sauce, cover, and bake for 1 hour or until chicken is tender.
- Meanwhile sauté almonds in butter until golden. Slice avocado and sprinkle with lemon juice.
- Place chicken on individual plates. Spoon over sauce.
- Top with avocado slices and slivered almonds.

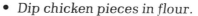

Avocado and Honey-Glazed Chicken

serves six

6 chicken breasts (boned)
3 tablespoons wholemeal flour
2 tablespoons butter
1 medium onion (chopped)
½ cup chicken stock
3 tablespoons honey
1 tablespoon orange rind (finely grated)
½ teaspoon paprika
    sea salt and freshly ground black pepper to taste
3 medium avocados (peeled, halved and stoned)
1 tablespoon lemon juice

- Dip chicken pieces in flour.
- In a large frying pan, brown chicken pieces in melted butter, then remove.
- Sauté the onion in the butter remaining in the frying pan until transparent.
- Return chicken to pan and add chicken stock.
- Combine honey and grated orange rind and brush onto chicken pieces. Sprinkle with paprika, sea salt and pepper.
- Cover pan and simmer for 1 hour.
- Prepare avocados and sprinkle with lemon juice.
- Brush chicken pieces again with honey and grated orange rind. Cover and simmer for five more minutes.
- Place chicken pieces on avocado halves and spoon over the onions and pan juices. Serve immediately.

Peachy Chicken

serves six

6   chicken breasts
3   tablespoons wholemeal flour
2   tablespoons butter
1   medium onion (thinly sliced)
1   cup peach nectar
     sea salt and freshly ground black pepper to
     taste
1   large avocado

- Dip chicken pieces in flour.
- Melt butter in a large frying pan and brown chicken pieces.
- Add onion rings, peach nectar, sea salt and pepper; cover and simmer for 1 hour or until tender.
- Peel, stone and slice avocado.
- Place chicken on individual plates. Spoon over peach sauce.
- Garnish with avocado slices.

Lemon Chicken

serves six

6 chicken breasts
3 tablespoons wholemeal flour
2 tablespoons butter
½ cup chicken stock
   Lemon Sauce (see below)
1 large avocado (peeled, stoned and sliced)

- Preheat oven to 175°C (350°F).
- Dip the chicken pieces in flour and brown in butter in frying pan. Place chicken in baking dish and add chicken stock.
- Baste chicken with lemon sauce. Cover and bake for one hour or until chicken is tender. Baste occasionally with lemon sauce.
- Serve chicken pieces on individual plates topped with slices of avocado.

Lemon Sauce

8 tablespoons lemon juice
2 cloves garlic (crushed)
1 tablespoon grated lemon rind
1 tablespoon grated onion
1 tablespoon parsley (finely chopped)

- Combine all ingredients and mix well.

Roast Duck with Orange and Avocado Sauce

serves six

1 2kg duck (4½lb)
2 cups breadcrumbs
2 tablespoons parsley (chopped)
1 medium onion (finely chopped)
1 tablespoon shallots (chopped)
1 teaspoon sage
   sea salt and freshly ground pepper to taste
250 g (½ lb) sausage meat or finely minced giblets
1 egg
   slice of orange
4 tablespoons wholemeal flour
2 tablespoons bacon fat
   Orange and Avocado Sauce (see below)

- Preheat oven to 175°C (350°F).
- Combine breadcrumbs, parsley, onion, shallots, sage, sea salt and pepper in a mixing bowl.
- Knead the sausage meat into the mixture and then stir in the raw egg.
- Put the stuffing into the cleaned body of the bird and seal with the slice of orange.
- Sprinkle the flour into the bottom of a baking dish. Place the stuffed bird in baking dish and baste with bacon fat.
- Cover bird with aluminium foil and place in oven for 1¼ hours. Remove foil and cook for further 40 minutes to brown.
- Serve with orange and avocado sauce.

Orange and Avocado Sauce

2 chicken stock cubes
½ teaspoon vegemite
1 orange
2 cups water
   sea salt and freshly ground black pepper to taste
2 tablespoons curacao
1 small avocado (peeled, stoned and diced)

- Peel orange rind thinly and dice finely. Cut orange into segments.
- Combine chicken stock cubes, vegemite, orange rind, orange segments, water, sea salt, pepper, and curacao. Boil all together, (uncovered) for 25 minutes.
- Just before serving, turn down heat, stir in avocado gently and serve immediately.

Tahmoor Turkey

serves six

¼   cup onion (chopped)
½   cup celery (chopped)
2   tablespoons butter
1½ cups turkey (cooked and diced)
1   cup potatoes (cooked and diced)
1   cup chicken or turkey stock
    sea salt and freshly ground black pepper to
    taste
1   large avocado (peeled, stoned and sliced)
6   slices wholemeal bread (toasted)

- Sauté onion and celery in butter until onions are transparent.
- In a saucepan, combine turkey, potatoes, celery, onion, chicken stock, sea salt and pepper. Simmer for five minutes.
- Arrange avocado slices on top of toast. Place on individual plates. Spoon over turkey hash and serve immediately.

Tashi Chicken

serves four

2 tablespoons butter
3 tablespoons shallots (chopped)
1½ cups chicken (cooked and sliced)
½ cup chicken stock
2 tablespoons parsley (finely chopped)
1 tablespoon soy sauce
1 cup lychees (halved)
2 cups brown rice (cooked)
1 medium avocado (peeled, stoned and diced)
  paprika

- Melt butter in frying pan. Add shallots and sauté until shallots are transparent.
- Add chicken, chicken stock, parsley and soy sauce. Simmer for ten minutes. Add lychees and simmer for further five minutes.
- Serve on a beds of rice, garnished with diced avocado. Sprinkle with paprika.

Tempura

serves four

Batter

½ cup cauliflower pieces
1 medium onion (quartered and divided into wedges)
1 small avocado (peeled, stoned and sliced)
1 capsicum (cut into chunks)
½ cup broccoli pieces
12 king prawns (cooked and cleaned)
   batter (see below)
   safflower oil
   guacamole (page 11)

- Prepare cauliflower, onion, avocado, capsicum, broccoli and king prawns.
- Heat oil to moderately hot. Dip the ingredients in batter and deep fry until golden.
- Remove ingredients from oil, drain on brown paper or kitchen towelling, and keep warm in oven.
- Serve immediately with guacamole.

1 egg (separated)
6 tablespoons beer
⅓ cup plain flour
½ teaspoon dry mustard
½ teaspoon sea salt
⅛ teaspoon freshly ground black pepper

- Combine beaten egg yolk, beer, plain flour, dry mustard, sea salt and pepper. Beat with an egg beater until ingredients are well mixed.
- Beat egg white until stiff and fold into other ingredients

Avocado Lobster Newburg

serves four

4-6 slices wholemeal bread
  3 tablespoons butter
  2 tablespoons wholemeal flour
  ¾ cup cream
  2 egg yolks (beaten)
  2 tablespoons sherry
  1 cup lobster (cooked and cut into bite-size pieces)
  ½ teaspoon paprika
     sea salt and freshly ground black pepper to taste
  1 large avocado (peeled, stoned and sliced)

- Toast bread and cut each piece into three strips.
- Melt butter in saucepan. Remove saucepan from stove and stir in flour to make a smooth paste. Cook, stirring, over low heat for 2 to 3 minutes.
- Add cream and stir over a low heat until mixture begins to thicken.
- Add beaten egg yolks, sherry, lobster, paprika, sea salt and pepper, stirring constantly.
- Heat for a few minutes, then spoon over slices of avocado placed on strips of toast.

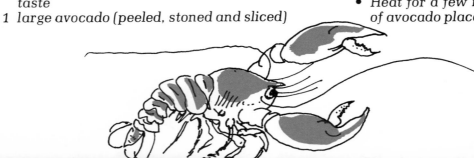

Prawn Curry

serves six

3 tablespoons safflower oil
1 tablespoon curry powder
1 tablespoon ground coriander
¼ teaspoon chili powder (or more, to taste)
4 large onions (chopped)
1½ cups chicken stock
1 teaspoon sea salt
1½ cups prawns (cooked and cleaned)
3 cups brown rice (cooked)
1 large avocado (peeled, stoned and diced)
1 tablespoon lemon juice

- Combine safflower oil, curry powder, coriander and chili powder in a frying pan. Mix well.
- Heat oil and curry mixture, add chopped onions and cook until onions are transparent.
- Add chicken stock and sea salt, remove from heat, and allow to stand at room temperature for four hours or longer.
- Add prawns and reheat for 5 or 6 minutes.
- Combine rice, avocado and lemon juice. Mix gently, and spoon onto individual plates.
- Spoon prawn curry over rice and avocado.
- Serve with side dishes of chopped nuts, chopped tomato and onion, chutney, bananas sprinkled with coconut, chopped cucumber in yoghurt, sultanas, and so on.

Avocado Creole

serves four

2   rashers bacon
¼   cup green capsicum (chopped)
½   cup celery (chopped)
1   medium onion (chopped)
1   cup tinned tomatoes
3   tablespoons tomato paste
½   teaspoon raw sugar
½   teaspoon chili powder
1   cup school prawns (cooked and cleaned)
2   cups brown rice (cooked)
1   medium avocado (peeled, stoned and diced)
1   tablespoon lemon juice

- Fry bacon in frying pan until crisp. Remove and drain on brown paper or kitchen towelling.
- Add green pepper, celery and onion to bacon fat and cook until onions are transparent.
- Add tomatoes, tomato paste, raw sugar and chili powder, and simmer gently for 30 minutes.
- Cook brown rice and mix with diced avocado and lemon juice.
- Add prawns to tomato mixture, heat, and serve over rice and avocados. Garnish with crumbled bacon.

Jambalaya

½ cup brown rice
2 cups water
1 medium onion (chopped)
1 clove garlic (finely chopped)
2 tablespoons butter
½ cup chicken broth
⅓ cup celery (chopped)
½ cup tomatoes (peeled and chopped)
1 bay leaf
¼ teaspoon oregano
   pinch of thyme
1 teaspoon chili sauce
½ cup prawns (cooked and cleaned)
½ cup ham (cooked and diced)
2 avocados (peeled, stoned and halved)
   sea salt and freshly ground black pepper to
   taste

- Boil 2 cups of water in saucepan. Add rice, cover and simmer for 25 minutes or until tender. Drain and put aside.
- Sauté onion and garlic in butter until onions are transparent.
- Add chicken broth, celery, tomatoes, bay leaf, oregano, thyme, salt, pepper and chili sauce. Cover and simmer gently for ½ hour.
- Add rice, prawns, and ham; heat and serve over avocado halves.

Crab Yarramundi

serves four

    3   tablespoons shallots (finely chopped)
    1   tablespoon butter
    ¾   cup cream
    ½   cup ambrosia cheese (grated)
    ¾   cup crab meat
    ¼   teaspoon sea salt
        pinch of cayenne pepper
    2   avocados (peeled, stoned, halved and
        sprinkled with lemon juice)
        parsley

- Sauté shallots in butter until golden.
- Add cream, cheese, crab meat, sea salt and cayenne pepper.
- Simmer gently for five minutes.
- Spoon over avocados and garnish with parsley.

Hamburger with Tomato Relish

serves four

2 cups topside mince
  tomato relish
1 medium avocado (peeled, stoned and sliced)
4 wholemeal buns
2 tablespoons butter
1 tablespoon oil

- Make four hamburger patties with mince. Put oil in skillet, heat, add hamburger patties and cook on medium heat, turning occasionally, for 15-20 minutes.
- Meanwhile halve buns, butter and toast under griller.
- Drain hamburgers and place on bottom half of buns.
- Place avocado slices on hamburgers. Top with tomato relish.

Avocado Burgers

serves four

1   medium avocado (peeled, stoned and mashed)
1   cup cooked soybeans
6   shallots (finely chopped)
3   tablespoons tomato paste
1   tablespoon celery (finely chopped)
1   clove garlic (crushed)
1   tablespoon parsley
½   cup breadcrumbs
4   tablespoons sesame oil

- Combine avocado, soybeans, shallots, tomato paste, celery, garlic and parsley.
- Mix well and shape into patties. Turn patties in breadcrumbs and fry in oil until browned.

Tacos with Guacamole

serves four to six

```
12   tortilla shells (fried and ready to use)
 1   onion (chopped)
 2   tablespoons safflower oil
450  g (1lb) mince meat
 1   small tin tomato paste
 1   tablespoon chili sauce
 ¼   teaspoon oregano
     small head of lettuce (shredded)
 ½   cup cheddar cheese (grated)
12   tablespoons sour cream
     Guacamole (see page 11)
```

- Fry onion in oil until golden. Add mince meat and brown.
- Add tomato paste, chili sauce and oregano. Simmer for 20 minutes.
- Warm tortilla shells.
- Put meat, tomato, lettuce, cheese and sour cream into tortilla shells.
- Top with guacamole.

Tostados

serves four

4   tortillas
1   cup refried beans (see below)
1   cup shredded lettuce
¾   cup mince meat filling (see below)
¾   cup cheddar cheese (grated)
1   large avocado (peeled, stoned and sliced) or 1
    cup guacamole (see p. 11)
½   cup chili sauce (see below)

- Fry tortillas in hot vegetable oil.
- Heat refried beans and spread over tortillas.
- Spoon on lettuce, meat filling, grated cheddar cheese and top with avocado slices. Serve with chili sauce.

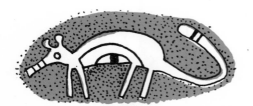

Refried Beans

½   cup dried pink or kidney beans
1   medium onion (chopped)
2   tomatoes (peeled and chopped)
4   tablespoons lard
    sea salt and freshly ground black pepper to taste

- Soak beans in water overnight. Rinse and place in a heavy saucepan with 2 cups water.
- Add onion, tomatoes, sea salt and pepper and bring to a boil. Reduce heat and simmer slowly for 2½ hours or until beans are tender. Mash beans with a potato masher (or a fork).
- Melt lard in a frying pan and add beans. Cook until beans absorb lard.

Meat Filling

1 cup minced steak
1 medium onion (chopped)
6 tablespoons chili sauce (see below)
1 tablespoon oil

- Brown mince meat and onion in oil. Add chili sauce and simmer for half an hour.

Chili Sauce

3 large tomatoes (peeled and chopped)
1 medium onion (chopped)
1 clove garlic (finely chopped)
2 tablespoons butter
1 tablespoon chili powder (or to taste)
¼ teaspoon mustard seeds (crushed)
2 tablespoons vinegar
1 teaspoon honey

- Sauté onion and garlic in butter until golden.
- Add tomatoes, mustard seeds, chili powder, vinegar and honey. Simmer gently for an hour.
- Force chili sauce through a sieve with the back of a spoon.

Texican Chili Con Carne

serves six

2   cups round steak (cut into small cubes)
2   tablespoons wholemeal flour
1   medium onion (peeled and chopped)
3   cloves garlic (finely chopped)
2   tablespoons lard
1   cup beef stock
2   teaspoons chili powder (or more or less to taste)
1   teaspoon whole cumin
2   tablespoons parsley (chopped)
½   teaspoon oregano
½   teaspoon sea salt
1   cup cooked red beans
3   avocados (peeled, halved and stoned)

- Roll beef in flour and brown with onions and garlic in lard.
- Add beef stock, chili powder, cumin, parsley, oregano and sea salt. Cover and simmer for one hour.
- Add red beans and cook for further 8 to 10 minutes.
- Prepare avocados and spoon chili con carne over them.

Odds and Ends

Side Salads
Vegetable Dishes
Sauces
Desserts
Drinks
Cosmetics

Green Salad

1 head lettuce
¼ cup green capsicum
1 avocado (peeled, stoned and sliced)
1 cucumber (sliced)
4 artichoke hearts (quartered)
½ cup seedless green grapes
2 tablespoons parsley (chopped)
  Dressing (see below)

- Tear lettuce into bite-size pieces and cut capsicum into strips.
- Combine lettuce and capsicum with avocado and cucumber slices, artichoke hearts, grapes and parsley in a salad bowl.
- Toss with dressing and serve.

Dressing

2 tablespoons olive oil
2 tablespoons white vinegar
2 tablespoons tomato sauce
½ teaspoon onion salt
2 drops Tabasco sauce
1 teaspoon raw sugar
2 teaspoons lemon juice

- Combine ingredients in a jar and shake well.

Avocado with Best Dressing

serves six

2 avocados
1 head lettuce
   Best Dressing (see below)

- Peel, stone and slice avocados.
- Arrange avocado slices on beds of lettuce and pour dressing over.

Best Dressing

2 tablespoons olive oil
2 tablespoons vinegar
2 tablespoons tomato sauce
2 teaspoons raw sugar
1 tablespoon shallots (finely chopped)
1 clove garlic (crushed)
1 tablespoon lemon juice
   sea salt and freshly ground black pepper to taste

- Combine all ingredients and beat thoroughly with an egg beater.

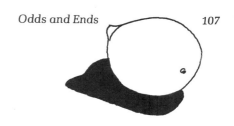

Tomato and Onion Salad

1 large avocado (peeled, stoned and sliced)
1 large tomato (sliced)
1 small onion
1 head lettuce
2 tablespoons parsley (chopped)
  Dressing (see below)

- Peel onion, slice thinly and separate into rings.
- Arrange avocado slices and tomato slices alternately on a bed of lettuce.
- Garnish with onion rings and parsley.
- Pour over dressing.

Dressing

2 tablespoons oil
1 teaspoon apple cider vinegar
1 tablespoon lemon juice
1/8 teaspoon garlic powder
  vegetable salt and freshly ground black pepper to taste

- Combine all ingredients in a jar and shake well.

Red Pepper Salad

1 red capsicum
1 avocado (peeled, stoned and sliced)
1 medium cucumber (peeled and sliced)
1 head lettuce
½ cup nuts (chopped)
   Dressing (see below)

- Remove seeds from capsicum and cut into narrow circles.
- Arrange capsicum, avocado and cucumber slices on a bed of lettuce.
- Pour dressing over and top with chopped nuts.

Dressing

1 tablespoon olive oil
1 tablespoon white vinegar
1 tablespoon tomato sauce
½ teaspoon onion salt
2 drops Tabasco sauce
1 teaspoon raw sugar
1 teaspoon lemon juice

- Combine all ingredients in a jar and shake well.

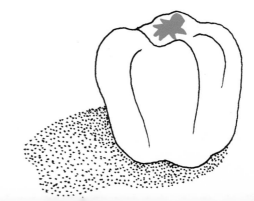

Mazatlan Salad

1 large avocado (peeled, stoned and sliced)
2 small tomatoes (cut into wedges)
2 tablespoons shallots (finely chopped)
8 stuffed olives (halved)
4 artichoke hearts (quartered)
1 head lettuce
½ cup garlic croutons
Dressing (see below)

- Tear lettuce into bite-size pieces and combine with sliced avocado, tomatoes, chopped shallots, olives, artichoke hearts and garlic croutons in a salad bowl.
- Toss with dressing.

Dressing

3 tablespoons safflower oil
1 teaspoon chili sauce
1 tablespoon lemon juice
1 garlic clove (crushed)
   sea salt and freshly ground black pepper to taste

- Combine all ingredients in a jar and shake well.

Sunshine Salad

2 oranges (peeled, seeded and chopped)
1 avocado (peeled, stoned and sliced)
1 small onion (peeled, thinly sliced and divided
   into rings)
1 head lettuce
   Honey and Lemon Dressing (see below)

- Combine chopped oranges, avocado slices and
  onion rings in a bowl and mix gently.
- Spoon orange and avocado salad onto a bed of
  lettuce on a salad platter.
- Pour over dressing.

Honey and Lemon Dressing

4 tablespoons safflower oil
2 teaspoons honey
2 tablespoons lemon juice
1 teaspoon orange rind (grated)
   sea salt to taste

- Combine all ingredients in a jar and shake well.

Avocado Bacon Salad

2   slices wholemeal bread
2   tablespoons butter
1   clove garlic (crushed)
1   small head of lettuce
1   avocado (peeled, stoned and diced)
3   rashers bacon
1   cup cherry tomatoes (halved)
¼   cup cheddar cheese (grated)
    Dressing (see below)

- Remove crusts from bread and cut into cubes. Sauté in butter with crushed garlic until golden brown. Drain on brown paper or kitchen towelling.
- Grill bacon until crisp, drain and crumble when cool.
- Tear lettuce into bite-size pieces and combine in a salad bowl with avocado, tomatoes, bacon and cheese.
- Toss salad gently with dressing and top with garlic croutons.

Dressing

4   tablespoons olive oil
2   tablespoons white vinegar
2   teaspoons honey
½   teaspoon garlic powder
    freshly ground black pepper to taste

- Combine all ingredients in a jar and shake well.

Millionaires' Salad

serves six

Vinaigrette Dressing

1 large avocado (peeled, stoned and sliced)
1 tin hearts of palm (halved)
1 tin artichoke hearts (quartered)
1 head lettuce
½ cup cherry tomatoes
   Vinaigrette Dressing (see below)

- Halve hearts of palm and quarter artichoke hearts.
- Place hearts of palm, avocado and artichoke hearts on a bed of lettuce on a salad platter.
- Pour over dressing.
- Garnish with cherry tomatoes.

1 egg yolk
2 tablespoons vinegar
4 tablespoons olive oil
½ teaspoon French mustard
1 teaspoon lemon juice
¼ teaspoon raw sugar
1 clove garlic (crushed)
   sea salt and freshly ground black pepper to taste

- Beat egg yolk with vinegar. Gradually add oil, stirring vigorously.
- Add remaining ingredients and mix thoroughly.

Pecan Tango

1 avocado (peeled, stoned and sliced)
3 mandarins
2 teaspoons lemon juice
½ cup pecans (chopped)
1 head lettuce
   Tango dressing (see below)

- Peel mandarins, slice, remove seeds and chop.
- Combine avocado slices and chopped mandarins in a mixing bowl and sprinkle with lemon juice. Mix gently.
- Spoon mandarin salad onto a bed of lettuce on a salad platter.
- Top with pecans and pour dressing over.

Tango Dressing

3 tablespoons salad oil
1 tablespoon apple cider vinegar
¼ teaspoon dry mustard
½ teaspoon raw sugar
¼ teaspoon sea salt

- Combine all ingredients in a jar and shake well.

Dandelion Salad

1 cup tender dandelion leaves
½ cup bean sprouts
1 small head of lettuce
3 tablespoons parsley (chopped)
2 tomatoes (cut into wedges)
1 avocado (peeled, stoned and sliced)
2 tablespoons sunflower seeds
   Dressing (see below)

- Tear dandelion leaves and lettuce into bite-size pieces.
- Combine greens with bean sprouts, chopped parsley, tomato wedges, avocado slices and sunflower seeds in a salad bowl.
- Toss with dressing.

Dressing

3 tablespoons salad oil
1 tablespoon lemon juice
1 teaspoon apple cider vinegar
1 clove garlic (crushed)
1 teaspoon honey
   sea salt to taste

- Combine in a jar and shake well.

Matisse Salad

1 cup rockmelon balls
1 large tomato (sliced)
1 medium avocado (peeled, stoned and sliced)
   lettuce
   Dressing (see below)

- Halve rockmelon, remove seeds and scoop out flesh in balls.
- Arrange rockmelon balls, tomato slices, and avocado slices on a bed of lettuce on a salad platter.
- Pour over dressing and serve.

Dressing

2 tablespoons oil
1 tablespoon lemon juice
1 teaspoon mint (finely chopped)
½ teaspoon raw sugar

- Combine ingredients in a jar and shake well.

White Radish Salad

lettuce leaves
1 large avocado (peeled, stoned and sliced)
12 slices white radish
2 tomatoes (sliced)
8 capsicum rings
1 tablespoon chives (chopped)
French Dressing (page 121)

- On bed of lettuce leaves, arrange avocado slices, slices of white radish, slices of tomato and capsicum rings. Garnish with chives.
- Pour over French dressing.
- White radishes can be purchased at Chinese green grocers and are called daikon.

Green and White Salad

1   avocado (peeled, stoned and sliced)
1   cucumber (peeled and sliced)
     Sour Cream Dressing (see below)

- Toss avocado slices and cucumber slices with sour cream dressing.

Sour Cream Dressing

4   tablespoons sour cream
1   tablespoon shallots (finely chopped)
1   tablespoon lemon juice
½   teaspoon paprika
     pinch of cayenne pepper
     sea salt to taste

- Combine ingredients and mix thoroughly.

Green Grape Salad

serves four

2   avocados (halved and stoned)
½   lemon
¾   cup seedless green grapes
     Dressing (see below)

- Sprinkle avocado halves with lemon juice.
- Fill avocado cavities with green grapes, and pour over dressing.

Dressing

2   tablespoons safflower oil
2   teaspoons honey
2   tablespoons lemon juice
1   teaspoon orange rind (ggrated)

- Combine ingredients in a jar and shake well.

Vineyard Salad

1 small head of lettuce (torn into bite-size pieces)
2 medium tomatoes (sliced)
½ cup pineapple pieces
1 medium avocado (peeled, stoned and sliced)
¼ cup sultanas
2 apples (cored and sliced)
½ cup black grapes (halved)
Honey and Lemon Dressing (see below)

- *Combine lettuce, tomatoes, pineapple pieces, avocado slices, sultanas, apple slices, and black grapes in a salad bowl.*
- *Toss with dressing and serve.*

Honey and Lemon Dressing

4 tablespoons salad oil
2 teaspoons honey
1 clove garlic (crushed)
2 tablespoons lemon juice
2 teaspoons apple cider vinegar
  sea salt and freshly ground black pepper to taste

- *Combine ingredients in a jar and shake well.*

Grapefruit and Avocado Salad

serves four

1 medium avocado
1 pink grapefruit
   lettuce leaves
   French Dressing (see below)

- Peel, stone and slice avocado. Peel grapefruit and divide into segments.
- Place lettuce leaves on four salad plates.
- Arrange avocado slices and grapefruit sections alternately on lettuce. Pour over dressing.

French Dressing

2 tablespoons olive oil
2 tablespoons vinegar
2 tablespoons tomato sauce
2 teaspoons raw sugar
1 tablespoon shallots (finely chopped)
1 clove garlic (crushed)
1 tablespoon lemon juice
   sea salt and freshly ground black pepper

- Combine all ingredients and beat thoroughly with an egg beater.

Helen's Mushroom and Zucchini Salad

serves four to six

1 avocado (peeled, stoned and sliced)
1 cup mushrooms (sliced)
1 cup zucchinis (sliced)
2 teaspoons chopped parsley
   Dressing (see below)

- Marinate sliced avocado, mushrooms and zucchinis in dressing for one hour, turning occasionally.
- Serve garnished with chopped parsley.

Dressing

4 tablespoons safflower oil
1 tablespoon apple cider vinegar
   juice of ½ lemon
1 garlic clove (crushed)
½ teaspoon dry mustard
   sea salt and freshly ground black pepper to taste

- Mix all ingredients thoroughly.

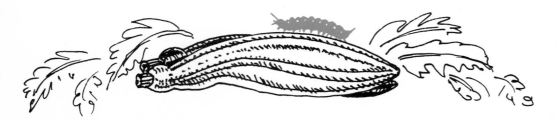

Southern Fried Avocado

1 large avocado (firm but ripe)
1 lemon
3 tablespoons wholemeal flour
2 eggs (well beaten)
4 tablespoons breadcrumbs
6 tablespoons safflower oil

- Peel, stone, and slice avocado. Sprinkle avocado slices with lemon juice. Dip slices in flour, then in egg, and then in breadcrumbs.
- Fry in hot oil in small pan for 15 seconds each side.

Twice Baked Potatoes

serves six

6 large potatoes
1 small avocado
6 tablespoons sour cream
2 tablespoons grated onion
1 teaspoon Worcestershire sauce
1 tablespoon lemon juice
  sea salt and freshly ground black pepper to taste
  breadcrumbs
3 tablespoons butter

- Bake potatoes in jackets at 230°C (450°F) for 1 hour. Pierce skin about half way through baking.
- Cut potatoes in half lengthwise and scoop out potato, being careful not to damage skin.
- Mash potatoes, and add mashed avocado, sour cream, grated onion, Worcestershire sauce, lemon juice, sea salt and pepper. Mix well.
- Spoon potato mixture into potato skins.
- Sprinkle breadcrumbs over potatoes. Top with a knob of butter.
- Brown in hot oven for 10 minutes.

Molokai Avocados

serves four

¼   cup onions (finely chopped)
¼   cup capsicum (finely chopped)
2   tablespoons butter
1   tomato (peeled and chopped)
½   cup mushrooms (sliced)
½   cup pineapple pieces (chopped)
    pinch of cayenne pepper
½   cup cheddar cheese (grated)
2   large avocados (halved and stoned)
1   tablespoon lemon juice
4   sprigs parsley

- Preheat oven to 175°C (350°F).
- Sauté onions and capsicum in butter for four to five minutes.
- Add tomatoes, pineapple, mushrooms and cayenne pepper and cook for five minutes, stirring occasionally.
- Add cheese and stir gently until cheese melts.
- Meanwhile, place avocado halves in a baking dish, sprinkle with lemon juice, and warm in oven for five minutes.
- Spoon pineapple mixture into avocado cavities, garnish with parsley, and serve immediately.

Marina Sauce

1   medium avocado (mashed)
1   tablespoon parsley (finely chopped)
1   tablespoon shallots (finely chopped)
2   tablespoons lemon juice
1   small tomato (peeled and chopped)
1   tablespoon capsicum (finely chopped)
1   clove garlic (crushed)
    sea salt and freshly ground black pepper to
    taste

- Combine mashed avocado, parsley, shallots, lemon juice, tomato, capsicum and garlic. Mix well. Season to taste with sea salt and pepper.
- This sauce can be served on a lettuce leaf next to grilled fish or can be spread over grilled fish just before serving.

Avocado Mayonnaise

2 egg yolks
1 tablespoon lemon juice
½ teaspoon sea salt
⅛ teaspoon freshly ground black pepper
¼ teaspoon dry mustard
1 small avocado (mashed)
1 teaspoon grated onion
2 teaspoons parsley (finely chopped)

- *Combine egg yolks, lemon juice, sea salt, pepper and dry mustard. Beat thoroughly with a whisk.*
- *Force mashed avocado through a sieve.*
- *Add avocado, onion and parsley to the egg mixture. Mix well.*
- *Use the same day as it does not keep.*

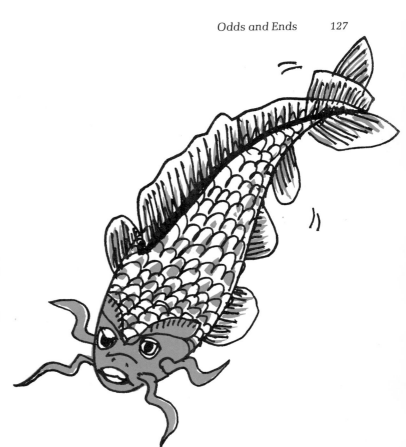

Avocado Sauce for Grilled Meats

1 large avocado (mashed)
1 tablespoon olive oil
1 teaspoon vinegar
1 teaspoon chili sauce
1 teaspoon onion (finely chopped)
¼ teaspoon ground coriander
1 tablespoon lemon juice
   sea salt and freshly ground black pepper to
   taste

- Combine olive oil, vinegar, chili sauce, chopped onion, coriander, lemon juice, sea salt and pepper. Mix well.
- Add mashed avocado to other ingredients and mix until well blended.
- Serve with grilled steak or lamb.

Fruit Salad Dressing

½ cup avocado purée
¼ cup whipped cream
1 tablespoon lemon juice
1 teaspoon grated orange rind
1 tablespoon honey

- *Combine avocado purée, lemon juice, grated orange rind and honey.*
- *Whip the cream until stiff. Add to avocado mixture and mix thoroughly.*

Crêpes

makes 8-10 crêpes

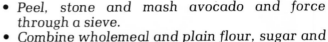

½ cup strained avocado
½ cup wholemeal flour (sifted)
1 dessertspoon plain flour
1 tablespoon raw sugar
¼ teaspoon sea salt
1 cup milk
2 tablespoons butter
1 tablespoon lemon juice
   safflower oil

- Peel, stone and mash avocado and force through a sieve.
- Combine wholemeal and plain flour, sugar and sea salt. Add beaten eggs, milk, melted butter, lemon juice and avocado.
- Beat well until batter is the consistency of slightly thickened cream. Add milk if necessary to thin. Cover and chill for one hour in refrigerator.
- Melt a little oil in a medium-size pan (preferably a crêpe pan). Pour in enough batter to cover the bottom of the pan, tipping the pan while adding the batter. Cook on each side until golden.
- Cover one half with filler and fold the other side over, or fold into three and pour sauce over.

Savoury Crêpe Filling

makes 8 crêpes

2 tablespoons butter
1 large onion (sliced and divided into rings)
3 medium tomatoes (peeled and sliced)
1 cup Mozzarella cheese (grated)

- Melt butter in saucepan. Add onion and tomato and cook gently for ten minutes.
- Add cheese and continue cooking until melted. Spoon onto crêpes.

Crêpes with Grand Marnier

serves four

4 crêpes
4 knobs of butter
   juice of ½ orange
4 tablespoons Grand Marnier

- Fold crêpes and put on warmed dessert plates.
- Place a knob of butter on each crêpe. Squeeze orange over each.
- Spoon over Grand Marnier, light, and serve.

Pineapple and Mint Salad

serves four

1 cup pineapple pieces (tinned or fresh)
1 tablespoon mint (finely chopped)
1 large avocado (peeled, stoned and sliced)
2 teaspoons lemon juice
  lettuce leaves
  watercress

- Drain pineapple and combine with mint in a bowl and mix well.
- Place avocado slices on a bed of lettuce and watercress; sprinkle with lemon juice.
- Spoon over pineapple and mint mixture and serve as a side salad.

Melon Salad

serves four

1 large avocado
1 small rockmelon (cut into balls)
2 cups watermelon (cut into balls)
   lemon juice
4 sprigs of mint

- Halve and stone avocado and scoop out flesh in balls.
- Scoop out balls of rockmelon and watermelon.
- Combine avocado, rockmelon and watermelon balls. Sprinkle with lemon juice. Chill.
- Place in glass bowls, garnish with mint, and serve.

Avocado Fruit Salad

serves six to eight

1 large avocado (peeled, stoned and diced)
2 oranges (peeled and divided into segments)
2 bananas (peeled and sliced)
1 cup strawberries (halved)
1 cup rockmelon (cut into balls)
1 cup honeydew melon (cut into balls)
1 cup pineapple pieces
1 cup peaches (peeled and sliced)
  juice of 1 lemon

- Combine avocado, oranges, bananas, strawberries, rockmelon, honeydew melon, pineapple and peaches in a bowl.
- Sprinkle lemon juice over fruit salad and toss.
- Chill and serve.

Sam's Fruit Salad

serves four

1 medium avocado (peeled, stoned and diced)
1 cup strawberries (halved)
1 cup pineapple pieces
½ cup cream
1 tablespoon castor sugar

- Sprinkle diced avocado with lemon juice.
- Combine avocado, strawberry halves and pine-apple pieces. Mix gently.
- Spoon into individual bowls. Chill for half an hour in the refrigerator.
- Whip cream, slowly adding castor sugar, until firm.
- Spoon whipped cream on top of fruit salad and serve.

Max's Mousse

serves six

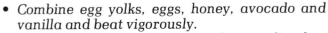

2 egg yolks
2 eggs
3 tablespoons honey
1 cup avocado purée
1 teaspoon vanilla essence
2 teaspoons gelatin
¼ cup hot water
2 tablespoons lemon juice
1 cup whipped cream
4 strawberries (halved)
1 kiwi fruit (peeled and sliced)

- Combine egg yolks, eggs, honey, avocado and vanilla and beat vigorously.
- Pour hot water over gelatin and stir to dissolve. Allow to sit for 15 minutes.
- Combine gelatin and avocado mixture. Mix well. Fold in whipped cream.
- Pour into mould which has been rinsed with cold water.
- Chill until set.
- Decorate with strawberry halves and sliced kiwi fruit (chinese gooseberries).

Avocado Snow

serves four

2 medium avocados (mashed)
4 teaspoons castor sugar
2 tablespoons lemon juice
2 egg whites

- Force mashed avocado through sieve.
- Add castor sugar and lemon juice and mix well.
- Beat egg white until stiff and fold into avocado mixture slowly.
- Place in bowls, chill and serve with thickened cream

Avocado Split

serves six

4 tablespoons pecans (toasted and chopped)
1 tablespoon butter
1 small avocado (mashed)
1 teaspoon honey
1 tablespoon lime juice
6 bananas (peeled and sliced lengthwise)

- Fry pecans in butter and let cool.
- Combine mashed avocado, honey and lime juice. Mix well.
- Place bananas on dessert plates. Spoon avocado mixture over bananas and top with chopped pecans.

Avocado Sherbert

serves six

2 teaspoons gelatin
1 cup fresh orange juice (save halved orange shells)
    juice of ½ lemon
1 teaspoon lemon rind (grated)
¾ cup raw sugar
2 egg whites (well beaten)
1 medium avocado (mashed)

- Boil 1 cup water. Remove from heat, add gelatin, stir to dissolve and let stand for 15 minutes.
- Combine orange juice, lemon juice, lemon rind, raw sugar, well beaten egg whites and avocado. Mix well.
- Combine gelatin and avocado mixtures in blender and mix until smooth.
- Put sherbert mixture into halved orange shells and freeze.

Peaches Ambrosia

serves four

4 peaches (peeled, halved and pitted)
1 small avocado (mashed)
1 tablespoon lemon juice
½ cup cream
1 tablespoon castor sugar
   chopped nuts

- Prepare peaches. Combine mashed avocado and lemon juice and spoon into peach hollows.
- Whip cream, slowly adding castor sugar, until firm. Spoon over peaches and avocado and top with chopped nuts.

Meringue Pie

serves six

1 *baked wholemeal pie shell*
¾ *cup milk*
4 *tablespoons honey*
2 *eggs*
2 *egg yolks*
1 *teaspoon vanilla essence*
1 *medium avocado (mashed)*
2 *egg whites*
¼ *cup castor sugar*

- *Preheat oven to 175⁰C (350⁰F).*
- *Combine milk, honey, well beaten eggs and egg yolks, vanilla and mashed avocado. Mix thoroughly.*
- *Pour mixture in pie shell.*
- *Beat egg whites until stiff. Then add sugar slowly while continuing to beat.*
- *Spoon meringue onto pie. Bake for 25 minutes or until meringue is golden.*

Avocado Cookies

      2 tablespoons butter
    ½ cup raw sugar
      1 medium avocado (mashed)
      2 egg yolks (well beaten)
    ¼ teaspoon sea salt
      1 teaspoon vanilla essence
      1 cup wholemeal flour
      1 tablespoon honey
    ½ cup walnuts

- Preheat oven to 190°C (375°F).
- Cream the butter and sugar together.
- Combine beaten egg yolks, mashed avocado, sea salt and vanilla essence. Mix well.
- Sift flour and add to avocado mixture. Add creamed butter and sugar, honey and walnuts. Mix well.
- Drop by teaspoonfuls onto greased baking sheet.
- Bake for 15 minutes and cool on a rack.

Avocado Banana Drink

serves four

1 medium avocado (peeled, stoned and diced)
1 cup banana (peeled and sliced)
1 cup milk
2 tablespoons raw sugar

- *Combine all ingredients in a blender and blend until smooth.*
- *Pour into four tall glasses.*

Avocado Egg Nog

serves six

1 small avocado (peeled, stoned and diced)
2 eggs (separated)
1 cup milk
1 tablespoon honey
3 tablespoons brandy
  nutmeg

- *Combine diced avocado, egg yolks, honey and milk in a blender. Blend until smooth.*
- *Beat egg whites until almost stiff and fold into avocado mixture.*
- *Add brandy and mix well. Pour into cocktail glasses and sprinkle nutmeg on top.*

Facial Cleanser

1   egg yolk
½   small avocado
1   tablespoon lemon juice

- Beat egg yolk thoroughly. Scoop out flesh of avocado and mash with fork.
- Combine egg, mashed avocado and lemon juice. Mix thoroughly into a smooth paste.
- Apply the cleanser to the face with cotton balls, avoiding eye area.
- Wipe away with gentle upward strokes, then pat face lightly with a face washer soaked in warm water.

Face Mask

2   egg whites
1   teaspoon lemon juice
1   small avocado

- Combine egg whites, lemon juice and mashed avocado. Mix well into a smooth paste.
- Apply generously with fingertips, avoiding the area around the eyes. Leave on your face for 15 minutes.
- Rinse thoroughly with luke-warm water.

Natural Moisturiser

1   avocado (skin only)

- Simply massage face with gentle upward strokes, using the inside of an avocado skin.
- Allow the natural oils to penetrate by waiting for about ten minutes, then rinse face thoroughly with warm water and pat dry with a soft face towel.

Index